MISSION
Greatness Spy

GS

By: Sarah How

MISSION
Greatness Spy

Publisher: How 2 Creative Services, 17550 200th Street, Audubon, MN 56511

Layout and Design: Copyright © 2025, How 2 Creative Services

Photographer: Justin How Productions - All photos used with permission.

All children included in the photographs were from 2024-2025 Kindergarten and Preschool classes at Zimmerman Elementary School in Wahpeton, ND and photographed with parent/caregiver permission.

EDUCATOR/CAREGIVER PAGE

We are grateful you chose *Mission Greatness Spy* to share with a child. We hope that each person reading this book will learn to spy greatness. Greatness reflects many different aspects of positive character qualities in ourselves and others. Once greatness is spied, the next step is learning to name the character quality a person shows by their actions. We hope everyone can celebrate greatness at school, home and in the community.

Learning about character qualities can be challenging for younger children unless these qualities are specifically described with experiences in a child's everyday life and environment. Teaching in this firsthand way helps children learn and understand new vocabulary and allows them to replicate positive choices and behaviors.

What is a Greatness Spy? A Greatness Spy is a person who uses their eyes to see and ears to hear all the positive greatness character qualities that children and adults show daily. In *Mission Greatness Spy*, each character quality is described in detail so a child can see, understand, speak about, and repeat positive behaviors. For example, when children are playing together, no one is arguing, and they are waiting their turn; they are showing the greatness of kindness, patience and self-control. On each mission page, there are mini-missions to teach children to see and speak about greatness. There is more than one greatness character quality in each picture. Invite children to describe what they see and have them name the greatness character words.

Let's be Greatness Spies with children. Our mission, just like theirs, is to find greatness and celebrate all the wonderful things that children and adults do daily. Together, we can make schools and the world a place where everyone is seen and belongs.

GREATNESS SPY TRAINING

Welcome to your mission. You will be going into training to be a Greatness Spy. Each page of this book is a new mission for you to learn and grow. Spying greatness is an important and special job. Your mission, Greatness Spy, is to look around your school and "spy" or see what someone is doing that is great and then tell them about their greatness. You will need to learn new greatness words to complete each mission. In Missions 1-9, you will be given greatness words to help you. Starting with Mission 10, you will use your own words. If you need help, go to the back of the book and find the Greatness Spy Words pages.

To complete each mission, you will need to ask yourself two special questions.

1. What is the person doing that is great?
2. What does that show you about who they are?

After you answer these questions, you complete each mission. There are 29 Missions in total.

On each page, you will see the Greatness Spy Seal telling you greatness has been spied.

Are you ready? Your mission starts now. Go Greatness Spy!

MISSION #1
YOUR MISSION HAS BEGUN!

I will go first then it is your turn. Start looking for greatness.

I spy **greatness**. Can you?

I see a child starting their day at school by greeting their helpers with smiles and high fives.

I spy the greatness of **friendliness** and **belonging**.

What **greatness** do you spy?

Ask yourself what is the person doing?
Now ask yourself what does that show you about who they are?

Greatness qualities to help you on your mission:

helpful, welcoming, joyful.

MISSION #1

MISSION #2

I spy **greatness**. Can you?

I see a child walking by themselves into a classroom and a parent smiling.

I spy the greatness of **independence** and being **ready to learn.**

What **greatness** do you spy? What is the person doing? What does that show you about who they are?

Greatness qualities to help you on your mission: **bravery, confidence, happiness.**

MISSION #2

MISSION #3

I spy **greatness**. Can you?

I see a child with an educator learning to write letters and words.

I spy the greatness of **courage** and **patience**.

What **greatness** do you spy? What is the person doing? What does that show you about who they are?

Greatness qualities to help you on your mission: **focus, helpful, perseverance.**

MISSION #3

MISSION #4

I spy greatness. Can you?

I see a child and an adult playing with toys together. I see children building puzzles.

I spy the greatness of connection and play.

What greatness do you spy? What is the person doing? What does that show you about who they are?

Greatness qualities to help you on your mission: cooperation, imagination, independence.

MISSION #4

MISSION #5

I spy **greatness**. Can you?

I see a learner putting things in the lost and found.

I spy the greatness of **helpfulness** and **kindness**.

What **greatness** do you spy? What is the person doing? What does that show you about who they are?

Greatness qualities to help you on your mission: **caring, generosity, organization.**

MISSION #5

MISSION #6

I spy **greatness**. Can you?

I see an older student reading to children. Students are keeping their hands and feet to themselves.

I spy the greatness of **leadership** and **listening**.

What **greatness** do you spy? What is the person doing? What does that show you about who they are?

Greatness qualities to help you on your mission: **focus, self control, shared enjoyment.**

MISSION #7

I spy **greatness**. Can you?

I see a child and an educator helping when someone is hurt.

I spy the greatness of **caring** and being **sensitive to others' needs.**

What **greatness** do you spy? What is the person doing? What does that show you about who they are?

Greatness qualities to help you on your mission: **helpful, kindness, thoughtfulness.**

MISSION #7

MISSION #8

I spy **greatness**. Can you?

I see children playing together during Physical Education class.

I spy the greatness of **fun** and **teamwork**.

What **greatness** do you spy? What is the person doing? What does that show you about who they are?

Greatness qualities to help you on your mission: **listening, self-control, wise choices.**

MISSION #8

MISSION #9

I spy **greatness**. Can you?

I see children sounding out letters to make words.

I spy the greatness of **discipline** and **learning.**

What **greatness** do you spy? What is the person doing? What does that show you about who they are?

Greatness qualities to help you on your mission: **attentive, resourceful, risk-taking.**

MISSION #9

MISSION #10

I spy **greatness**. Can you?

I see children running and swinging.

I spy the greatness of **energy** and **playfulness**.

What **greatness** do you spy? What is the person doing? What does that show you about who they are?

MISSION #11

I spy **greatness**. Can you?

I see children learning to count with shapes and blocks.

I spy the greatness of **persistence** and **problem-solving.**

What **greatness** do you spy? What is the person doing? What does that show you about who they are?

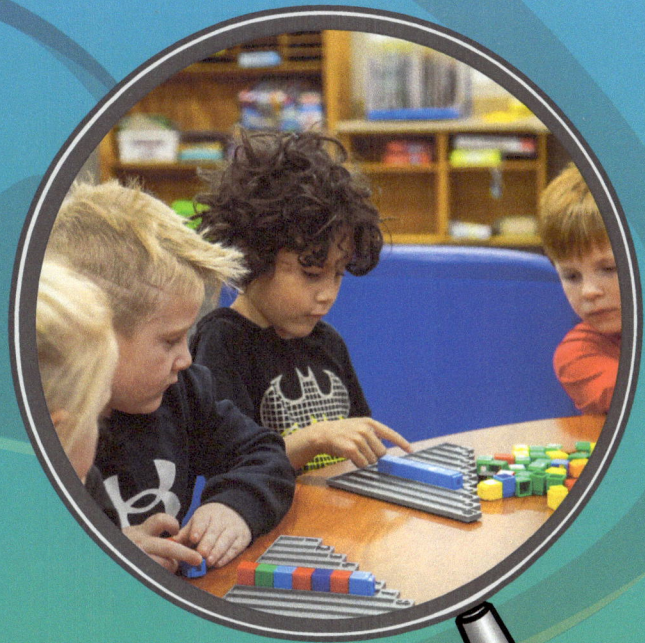

MISSION #11

MISSION #12

I spy **greatness**. Can you?

I see children and a teacher playing instruments and making music.

I spy the greatness of **creativity** and **musical expression.**

What **greatness** do you spy? What is the person doing? What does that show you about who they are?

MISSION #13

I spy **greatness**. Can you?

I see children writing words to make sentences.

I spy the greatness of **determination** and **risk-taking.**

What **greatness** do you spy? What is the person doing? What does that show you about who they are?

MISSION #13

MISSION #14

I spy **greatness**. Can you?

I see children getting water to drink and waiting for their turn. No one is pushing or budging in line.

I spy the greatness of **patience** and **politeness.**

What **greatness** do you spy? What is the person doing? What does that show you about who they are?

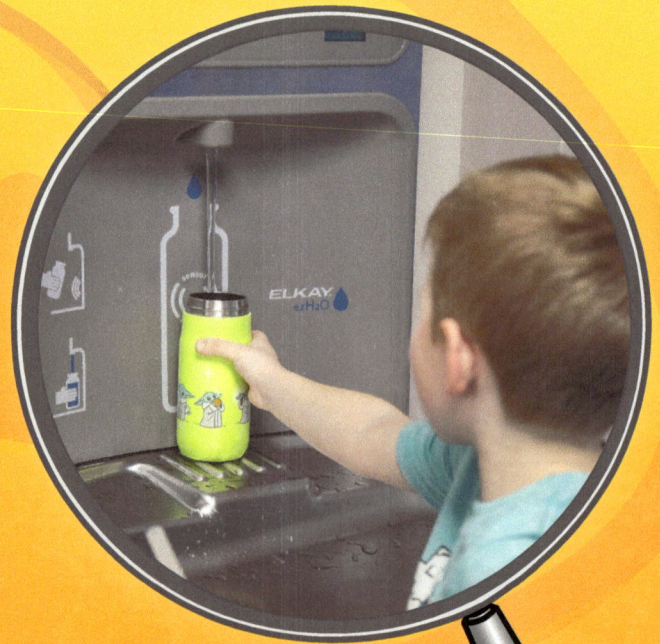

MISSION #14

MISSION #15

I spy **greatness**. Can you?

I see children lining up in the hall and walking with their voices off and hands to themselves.

I spy the greatness of **respect** and **self-control.**

What **greatness** do you spy? What is the person doing? What does that show you about who they are?

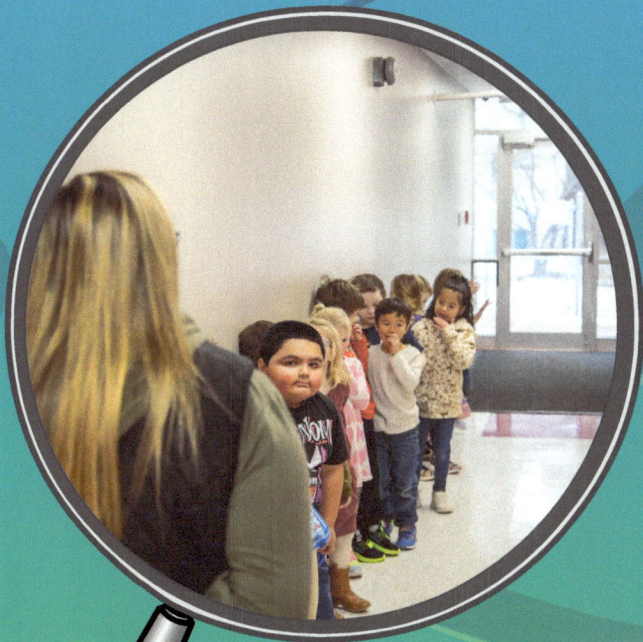

MISSION #15

MISSION #16

I spy **greatness** Can you?

I spy children washing their hands with soap and water to not spread germs.

I spy the greatness of **caring about others** and **cleanliness.**

What **greatness** do you spy? What is the person doing? What does that show you about who they are?

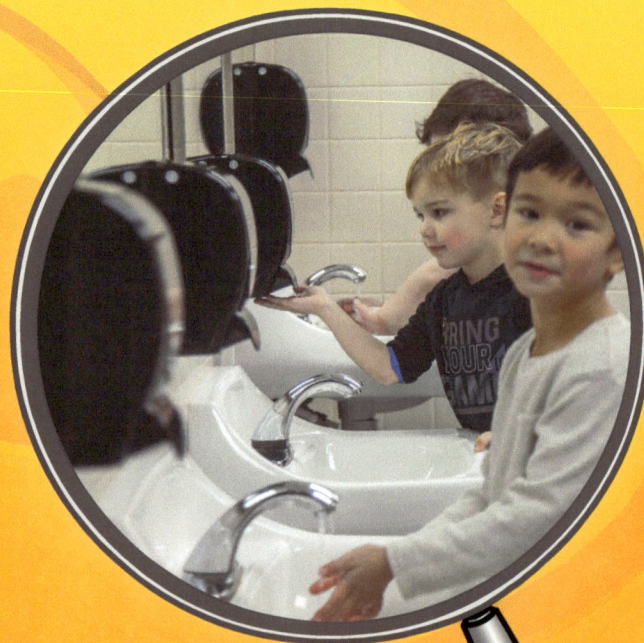

MISSION #17

I spy **greatness**. Can you?

I see children thanking school helpers for making them food.

I spy the greatness of **gratitude** and **thankfulness**.

What **greatness** do you spy? What is the person doing? What does that show you about who they are?

MISSION #17

MISSION #18

I spy **greatness**. Can you?

I see children sitting and eating together. They are smiling and talking.

I spy the greatness of **joyfulness** and **kindheartedness**.

What **greatness** do you spy? What is the person doing? What does that show you about who they are?

MISSION #18

MISSION #19

I spy **greatness**. Can you?

I see children learning about science with magnets.

I spy the greatness of **curiosity** and being **scientific.**

What **greatness** do you spy? What is the person doing? What does that show you about who they are?

MISSION #19

MISSION #20

I spy greatness. Can you?

I see children zipping their coats and getting their snow gear on all by themselves.

I spy the greatness of independence and perseverance.

What greatness do you spy? What is the person doing? What does that show you about who they are?

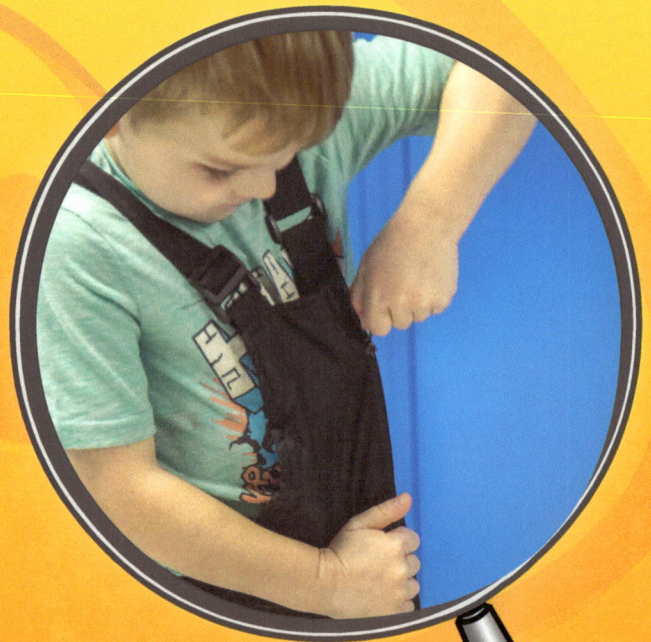

MISSION #21

I spy **greatness**. Can you?

I see children placing their bags, coats, and materials in their own space.

I spy the greatness of **organization** and **purposefulness**.

What **greatness** do you spy? What is the person doing? What does that show you about who they are?

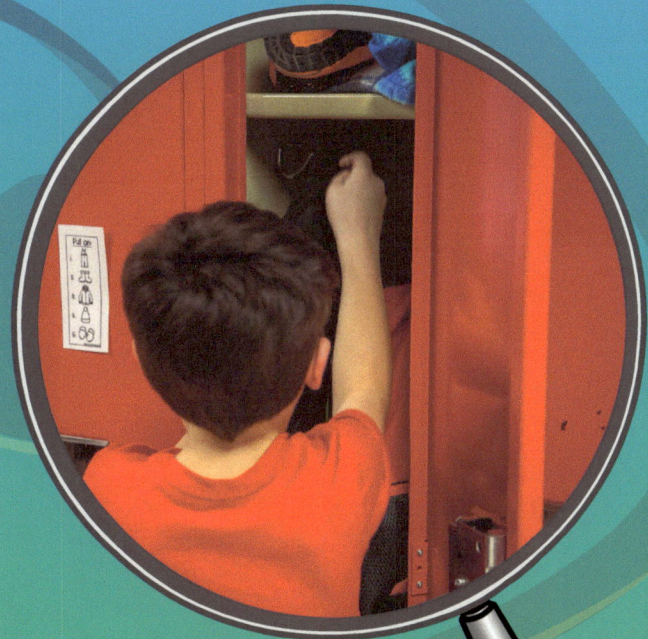

MISSION #21

MISSION #22

I spy **greatness**. Can you?

I see the school counselor working with children to take deep belly breaths when they are upset. They are not yelling or arguing.

I spy the greatness of **handling strong emotions** and being **teachable.**

What **greatness** do you spy? What is the person doing? What does that show you about who they are?

MISSION #22

MISSION #23

I spy **greatness**. Can you?

I see children building with blocks and working together.

I spy the greatness of **sharing** and **teamwork.**

What **greatness** do you spy? What is the person doing? What does that show you about who they are?

MISSION #23

MISSION #24

I spy **greatness**. Can you?

I see children making cards for the people in school who are helpers.

I spy the greatness of **appreciation** and **creativity**.

What **greatness** do you spy? What is the person doing? What does that show you about who they are?

MISSION #24

MISSION #25

I spy **greatness**. Can you?

I see children working with their hands to learn new skills.

I spy the greatness of **attentiveness** and **determination**.

What **greatness** do you spy? What is the person doing? What does that show you about who they are?

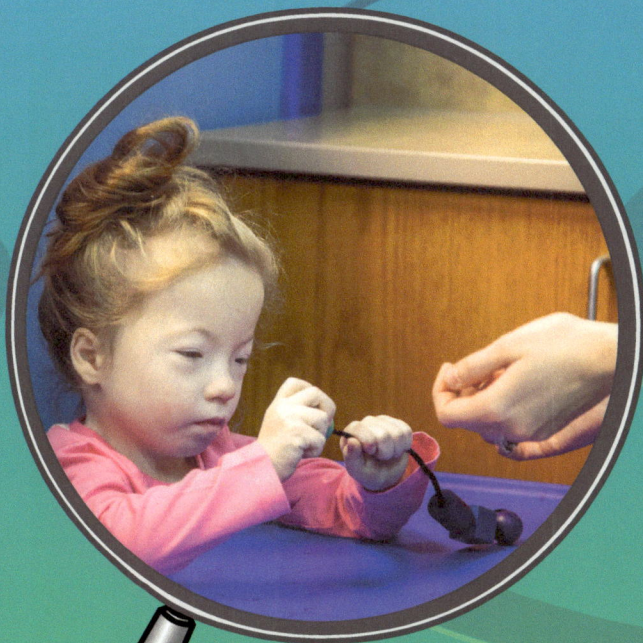

MISSION #25

MISSION #26

I spy **greatness**. Can you?

I see children coloring, drawing and making art.

I spy the greatness of being **artistic** and **creative**.

What **greatness** do you spy? What is the person doing? What does that show you about who they are?

MISSION #26

MISSION #27

I spy **greatness**. Can you?

I see children working with their teacher and reading together.

I spy the greatness of **using strategies** and **staying on-task together.**

What **greatness** do you spy? What is the person doing? What does that show you about who they are?

MISSION #27

MISSION #28

I spy greatness. Can you?

I see children teaching others strategies to learn.
They have calm bodies, quiet voices, listening ears and eyes watching their teacher.

I spy the greatness of being ready to learn and respect.

What greatness do you spy? What is the person doing? What does that show you about who they are?

MISSION #28

MISSION #29

I spy **greatness**. Can you?

I see children dancing and moving in their classrooms.

I spy the greatness of **fun** and **movement**.

What **greatness** do you spy? What is the person doing? What does that show you about who they are?

MISSION #29

MISSION
ACCOMPLISHED!

Congratulations! You spied greatness throughout this book. You are officially a Greatness Spy! Now it is time to go spy more greatness in your school and home.

Special thanks to all the educators and students at Zimmerman Elementary School in Wahpeton, North Dakota for showing us your greatness!

MISSION ACCOMPLISHED

EDUCATORS & CHILDREN

EDUCATORS & CHILDREN

EDUCATORS & CHILDREN

EDUCATORS & CHILDREN

A SPECIAL THANKS...

To my family, Mark, Kalob, Justin, Lydia and Chloe for supporting my great dreams. Chloe you show the greatness of love for choosing to work in special education at this school.

To Rose Hardie, Special Education Director, who cultivates greatness in all she does, and for trusting me with another children's book featuring her school district.

To Chandra Muller, Principal of Zimmerman Elementary, who easily spies greatness in children and educators. She graciously opened up her school and supported the work of sharing her students and educators with the world.

To a special student, Janiyah, who was featured on the cover of *Greatness Is My Superpower*. She willingly joined Mission #6 to show the greatness of leadership to younger children.

To Howard Glasser for creating the inspiring work of the Nurtured Heart Approach®.

THANK YOU!

GREATNESS SPY WORDS

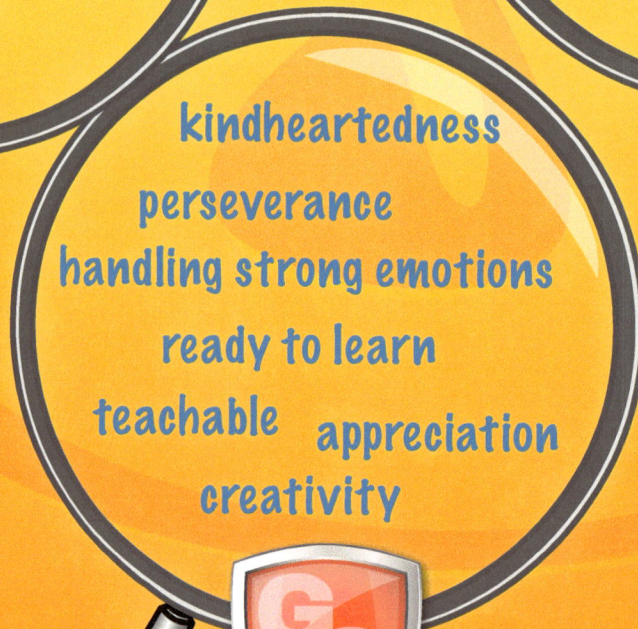

artistic

bravery

boldness

confidence

connection

independence

cooperation

joy

listening

self-control

wise choices

imagination

politeness

musical expression

cleanliness

caring about others

energy

kindheartedness

perseverance

handling strong emotions

ready to learn

teachable

appreciation

creativity

GREATNESS WORDS

risk-taking
curiosity
thoughtfulness
respect
kind
learning
hard-working
gratitude

patience
perseverance
determination
focus
helpful
organization
caring
generosity

attentiveness
purposefulness
staying on-task together
movement
scientific
teamwork
fun

GREATNESS WORDS

9 780989 340595